A

Science/Literature Unit

for

The Magic School Bus® Inside a Beehive

by Joanna Cole

Written by Ruth M. Young, M.S. Ed.

Teacher Created Materials, Inc.
P.O. Box 1040
Huntington Beach, CA 92647
©*1997 Teacher Created Materials, Inc.*
ISBN 1-57690-137-8
Made in U.S.A.

Illustrated by
Larry Bauer

Edited by
Walter Kelly

Cover Art by
Larry Bauer

Table of Contents

Introduction

The use of trade books can enhance the study of science. The key to selecting these books is to check them for scientific accuracy and appropriateness for the level of the students. *The Magic School Bus*® series, written by Joanna Cole, contains outstanding examples of books which can help students enjoy and learn about science. The series is delightfully written and scientifically accurate, thanks to the thorough research done by the author as she writes each of her books.

This Science/Literature Unit provides supplemental science activities related to *The Magic School Bus*® *Inside a Beehive.* These activities are particularly appropriate for intermediate grades. Teachers who use this unit will find a variety of lessons to do before, during, and after reading the book with their students. These lessons include the following:

- A Biographical Sketch
- A Book Summary
- Pre-reading Activities—sorting insects from non-insects
- Activity oriented lessons which relate to the topics covered in the story:

  Bees
  - Shadow puppet show about the life of honeybees
  - Dissecting flowers
  - Observing bees in the wild

  Ants
  - Observing ants in the wild
  - Drawing an ant from live specimens
  - Recording life in an ant farm

  Butterflies
  - Raising painted lady butterflies to observe the metamorphosis process

- Post-reading Activity/Assessment—Describing the process of becoming a bee, ant, or butterfly
- Annotated List of Books and Materials

The post-reading activity provides an open-ended question as assessment for the concepts students have gleaned from this unit. Another form of assessment is to have students make a collection or portfolio of the data sheets they use during their activities. Copies of the information pages used by the teacher may also be added. Let students use their artistic skills to create unique covers for their portfolios. These portfolios should be shared with parents at the end of the study and will serve as wonderful keepsakes for the students.

This unit is designed to help you present exciting lessons for your students so they can develop their understanding and appreciation of the insects found on Earth.

About the Author

Joanna Cole was born on August 11, 1944, in Newark, NY. She attended the University of Massachusetts and Indiana University before receiving her B.A. from the City College of the City University of New York in 1967. She has worked as an elementary library teacher, letters correspondent at *Newsweek,* and then became senior editor of books for young readers at Doubleday & Co.

Ms. Cole has written over 20 books for children, most of which are nonfiction. Every writer begins his or her career somewhere; Joanna Cole's began with cockroaches. While she was working as a library teacher in a Brooklyn elementary school, her father gave her an article about cockroaches, describing how they were on Earth before the dinosaurs. She had enjoyed reading science books as a child and remembered finding books about insects to be the most fascinating to her. Since there weren't any books about cockroaches, she decided to write one. Her first book, *Cockroaches,* was published in 1971.

Joanna Cole has written about fleas, dinosaurs, chicks, fish, saber-toothed tigers, frogs, horses, hurricanes, snakes, cars, puppies, insects, and babies, just to name a few examples. Ms. Cole knows that the important thing is to make the book so fascinating that the reader will be eager to go on to the next page.

Teachers and children have praised Ms. Cole's ability to make science interesting and understandable. Her *Magic School Bus*® series has now made science funny as well. Cole says that before she wrote this series, she had a goal to write good science books told in a story that would be so much fun that readers would read it even without the science.

Readers across the country love the *Magic School Bus*® series and enjoy following the adventures of the wacky science teacher, Ms. Frizzle. Joanna Cole works closely with Bruce Degen, the illustrator for this series, to create fascinating and scientifically accurate books for children. Even a successful writer finds it sometimes scary to begin writing a new book. That was the way Joanna felt before beginning to write the *Magic School Bus*® series. She says, "I couldn't work at all. I cleaned out closets, answered letters, went shopping—anything but sit down and write. But eventually I did it, even though I was scared."

Joanna Cole says kids often write their own *Magic School Bus*® adventures. She suggests they just pick a topic and a place for a field trip. Do a lot of research about the topic. Think of a story line and make it funny. Some kids even like to put their own teachers into their stories.

The Magic School Bus® Inside a Beehive

by Joanna Cole

(Scholastic, Inc., 1996)

(Canada, Scholastic; U.K., Scholastic Limited; AUS, Ashton Scholastic Party Limited)

Spring has come to Ms. Frizzle's class, and she has decided to arrange a special field trip for the students. She makes arrangements with a beekeeper to visit his hives. This fits right in with the study of insects her students are doing. Of course, you can be certain that this will not be the usual school field trip.

When the class arrives at the hives, they find the beekeeper is not there. Ms. Frizzle decides to serve the students a treat of honey while they wait for him. She accidentally drops the jar of honey, and suddenly the bus begins to vibrate and shrink. And, that's not all! The students and the Friz turn into bees! They go to the entrance of one of the hives, which is being guarded by the worker bees. Ms. Frizzle tells the students that if they find bee food from the flowers, the guards may let them enter the hive. They begin to fly and follow a bee to the flowers. There the students collect nectar and pollen.

Now, for the final touch. Ms. Frizzle sprays everyone with a special scent called *pheromone* so they can get past the guard. The guard bees smell them with their antennae and let them enter the hive.

Inside the hive, worker bees take the nectar and pollen from the students. They are now free to explore the hive. The first sight they see is the bee they had followed to the flowers, doing a special dance to show the other bees where the flowers are located.

The class finds the hive is covered with beeswax which the bees have shaped into a comb. These are hexagon cells that are used to raise the baby bees, store nectar and pollen, and make honey. The children even get to eat some of the tasty honey.

Suddenly, they notice the worker bees tending a huge bee. She is the queen bee! The queen bee moves from cell to cell, laying a small white egg in each one of them. The workers touch the queen with their antennae and lick and feed her.

Some cells have wormlike bee larvae in them. Nurse bees feed them. As they grow, they get too big for their skins and shed them; then they continue to eat and grow. Finally, each larva will spin a silk cocoon around itself and become a pupa. The nurse bees seal the cell with wax since the pupa does not eat. A great change, called *metamorphosis,* takes place as the pupa turns into the adult bee. When it emerges from its cocoon, it chews through the wax cell and joins the other bees.

Two queen bees emerge and fight until one bee kills the other. This new queen is pushed out of the hive, flies off, and mates with a drone bee. A new hive will now be formed.

Suddenly a bear attacks the hive, looking for the sweet honey. Ms. Frizzle and the children help save the hive by having the bear chase the bus. When they return to school, Ms. Frizzle and the students make delicious honey buns as a final treat. What a field trip!

Is This an Insect?

To the Teacher: This activity is a pre-assessment of the student's ability to recognize the characteristics which distinguish insects from other animals. At the end of the unit, repeat the activity as an assessment. Have the students write how they knew which were insects.

Materials: Insects and Non-Insects (page 7)

Lesson Preparation: Make copies of the pictures (page 7) on tagboard and cut them into individual sets for small groups of students to use. Make a transparency of the pictures and cut them into a set.

Procedure: Divide the students into groups of three or four and give each an envelope with a set of the pictures. Tell them to sort the pictures into insects and non-insects.

Closure: Discuss how each group sorted their pictures. Ask how they decided which pictures were of insects. Use the transparencies of the pictures to show the students the way the animals should be sorted. Share the Insect Facts with the students.

Answer Key for Insects and Non-Insects
(page 7)

> Insects have six legs and three body parts.

Insects	Non-Insects
	A—scorpion
B—honeybee	
C—ant	
D—stag beetle	
E—earwig	
	F—tarantula (spider)
G—grasshopper	
	H—centipede
I—butterfly	
	J—millipede
K—cockroach	
L—butterfly larva	

Is This an Insect? *(cont.)*

Insects and Non-Insects

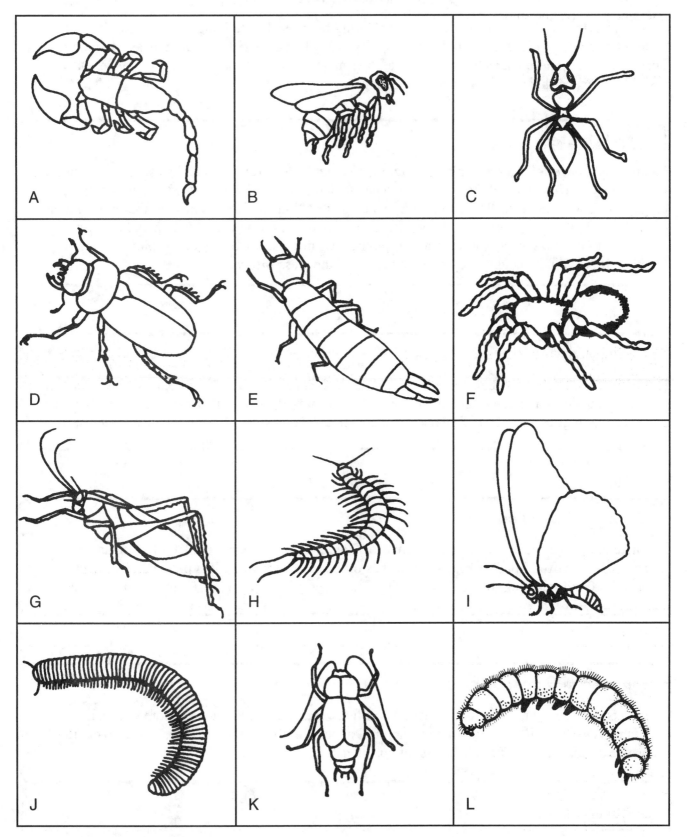

Is This an Insect? *(cont.)*

Insect Facts

Before studying bees, Ms. Frizzle has been preparing her class by studying all different kinds of insects. Naturally, she helps the students to learn the many special characteristics of insects as compared to other creatures. These characteristics include their main body parts, number of legs, range and distribution on earth, and relative age on the planet.

Invertebrates . . .

Insects are *invertebrates,* meaning that unlike mammals, fish, reptiles, and birds, they have no backbones. They have a hard, protective outer skeleton *(exoskeleton)* instead. Insects belong to a group of invertebrates called *arthropods*, which means "jointed foot." They are the only animals with three pairs of jointed legs. Most insects have two pairs of wings. Many people confuse other arthropods, such as spiders and scorpions, with insects. Spiders and scorpions have too many legs and not enough body parts to belong to the class *Insecta.*

Three Body Divisions . . .

Insects have three body divisions—*head, thorax,* and *abdomen.* The head contains the antennae, eyes (simple or compound), and mouth parts. The thorax is the middle body region to which the legs and wings are attached. The abdomen contains the digestive and reproductive systems.

800, 000 Species . . .

There are over 1 million species of animals on Earth, and more than 800,000 of these are insects. Scientists discover 7,000 to 10,000 new kinds of insects every year. It is predicted that there may be 1 to 10 million undiscovered species of insects. Insects live everywhere except in the ocean.

Older than Dinosaurs . . .

Insects have been on Earth for at least 400 million years, nearly 200 years before dinosaurs. Human's earliest ancestors did not appear until about 5 million years ago. Insects have obviously been extremely successful inhabitants of our planet.

Busy as a Bee

Ms. Frizzle is about to embark on another wildlife adventure with her class aboard the Magic School Bus®, of course. This time they plan to visit a beekeeper to see his beehives. We all know this will not be the normal school field trip!

To the Teacher: Familiarize the students with bees by sharing the Bee Facts with them and the picture of the Anatomy of a Worker Honeybee (page 10).

Bee Facts

Everywhere but the Poles . . .

Bees live in nearly every part of the world except the North and South Poles. They make honey, which people eat and beeswax, which is used in candles, adhesives, lipstick, chewing gum, and other useful things. Plants such as fruits and vegetables depend upon bees to pollinate them so they can reproduce seeds. As you can see, the bee is a very important and useful insect. There are about 20,000 different kinds of bees. Only the honeybee makes honey and wax.

80 Million Years Old . . .

Fossil bees have been found trapped in nectar and may have lived up to 80 million years ago. Bees most likely developed from wasplike ancestors that ate other insects. Gradually, they switched to flower nectar for their food. Scientists believe that bees have helped create a wide variety of flowering plants in the world, by spreading pollen among the plants.

Solitary and Social . . .

There are *solitary* bees and *social* bees. Most bees are solitary, such as the carpenter, leafcutting, mining, and mason bees. Solitary bees usually live alone while social bees live in colonies that have as few as 10 or as many as 80,000 members. Honeybees seem to have the most highly developed societies. Stingless bees and bumblebees are less social than honeybees. Stingless bees build nests in trees, on walls, in crude hives, or in the open. They may have from 50 to tens of thousands in their colonies. The bumblebee builds colonies of 50 to several hundred bees in the ground.

Busy as a Bee *(cont.)*

Anatomy of a Worker Honeybee

These detailed pictures show the body parts of a honeybee and explain their functions.

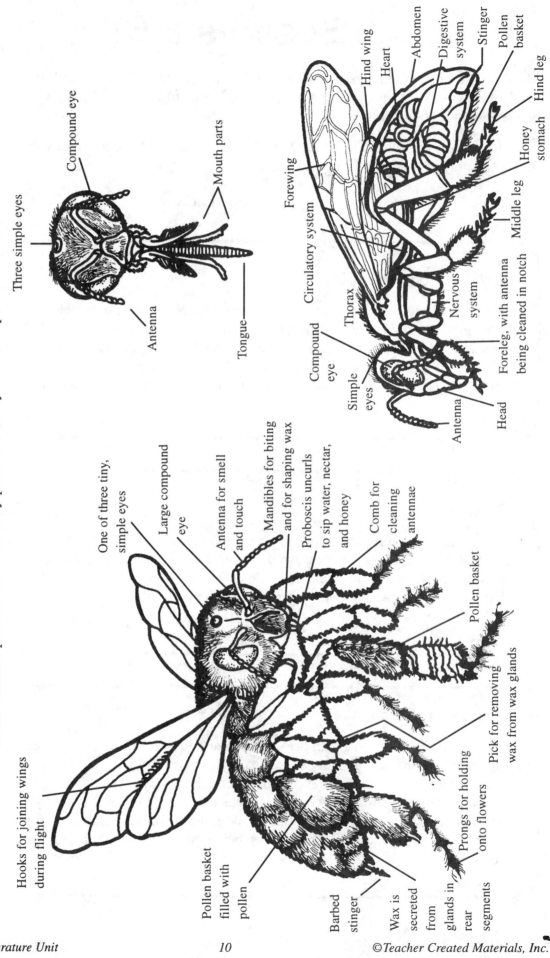

Compound eye

Three simple eyes

Antenna

Mouth parts

Tongue

Forewing

Hind wing

Heart

Abdomen

Digestive system

Stinger

Pollen basket

Hind leg

Honey stomach

Middle leg

Circulatory system

Nervous system

Foreleg, with antenna being cleaned in notch

Thorax

Compound eye

Simple eyes

Antenna

Head

One of three tiny, simple eyes

Large compound eye

Antenna for smell and touch

Mandibles for biting and for shaping wax

Proboscis uncurls to sip water, nectar, and honey

Comb for cleaning antennae

Pollen basket

Pick for removing wax from wax glands

Prongs for holding onto flowers

Wax is secreted from glands in rear segments

Barbed stinger

Pollen basket filled with pollen

Hooks for joining wings during flight

The Story of the Honeybee

To the Teacher: This activity is a shadow puppet show that simulates life in a honeybee colony. Only girls will read the roles, which are the queen and worker bees, since they are all female. The puppets can be handled by boys and girls. If there are not enough students for all the parts in the play, some may take more than one role as reader or puppeteer.

Readers Needed

(1) queen
(4) workers A, B, C, D
(3) scouts, A, B, C
(3) guards A, B, C
(1) stagehand for background transparencies
    (pages 14–17)

Puppets Needed

queen (1)
worker bees (4)
scout bees (3)
guard bees (3)
wasp (1)
top view of bee (1)

Materials: transparencies of puppets and scenery (pages 13–17); 14 feet (1.5 m) of 22 or 24 gauge wire; glue gun; orange, brown, and blue felt pens; puppet theater; overhead projector; large white butcher paper (*Wire may be purchased at a hardware or craft store.*)

Lesson Preparation: See page 12 for explanation and diagrams.

Procedure

- Select the script readers, puppeteers, and stagehand. Readers will read the script as the play unfolds. Puppeteers manipulate the puppets, holding them close to the screen to focus them and moving the puppets as suggested in the script. Directions are in italics to the left of the script.

- It will take practice for students to discover the right distance their puppets need to be from the screen so the image is in focus. They also need to learn how to stay low so shadows of their bodies are out of the light and only the puppets and background scenery cast shadows on the screen. Help students coordinate the action of their puppets and the scenery with the script.

Closure

- After the students have developed their skills in presenting the shadow puppet play, let them present it to the class.

- Rotate other students into the roles so they have the opportunity to participate.

Extender: Present the play to other classes in the school. Add background music, such as *The Flight of the Bumble Bee* or other appropriate music suggested by the story.

Let students add to the script, using information about bees from Bee Facts (page 9) or reference books (see Resources section).

The Story of the Honeybee *(cont.)*

Lesson Preparation: The shadow puppet stage may be created from a refrigerator box. Cut off the lids and one wide side of the box. Use the outer two sides as wings for the puppet theater. Cut a large rectangular hole near the top of the wide center panel and cover it with butcher paper. The paper becomes the screen for the puppet shadows. The audience sits on one side of the theater as the puppeteers work on the other (see drawing below). Transparencies of the scenery are placed on the stage of the overhead projector. Puppets are also made on transparencies which are then cut out and attached to a 12-inch (30 cm) length of wire.

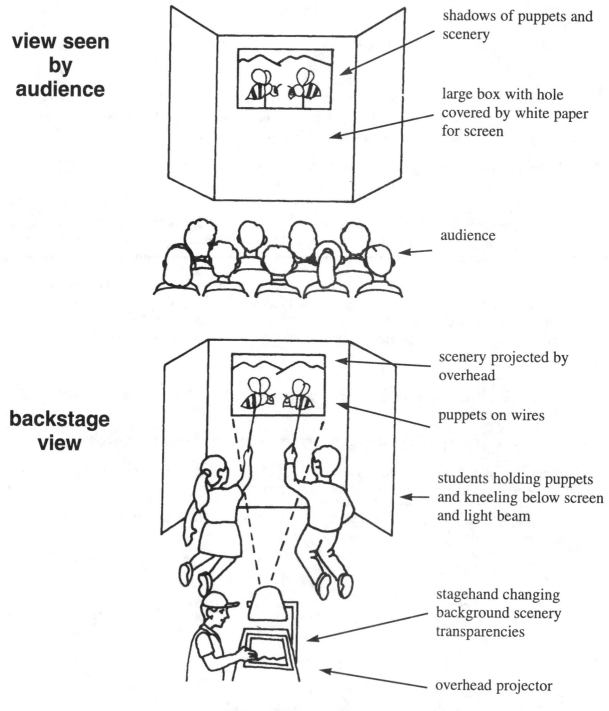

view seen
by
audience

shadows of puppets and scenery

large box with hole covered by white paper for screen

audience

backstage
view

scenery projected by overhead

puppets on wires

students holding puppets and kneeling below screen and light beam

stagehand changing background scenery transparencies

overhead projector

The Story of the Honeybee *(cont.)*

Bee Puppets

To the Teacher: Make transparencies of the puppets and cut them out without the captions. These are used only to identify the puppets for the puppeteer. The number of puppets needed for each picture is shown in parentheses beside the name.

Use the glue gun to attach the wire with tiny drops of hot glue to hold the puppets in a vertical position. The bees with wings that appear to be moving are used when they are flying during the play, such as the Scout A on page 20 of the script.

Queen (1)

Worker (4)

Drone (1)

Worker (1)
top view

Scout (3)

Wasp (1)

Guard (3)

The Story of the Honeybee *(cont.)*

Play Scenery

To the Teacher: Make transparencies of the scenery and cut them out to make individual pictures. Do not include captions which are to be used only in coordinating the pictures with the script. Prior to making transparencies, enlargement of these pictures may be needed to match the size of the puppets. This will prevent the necessity of changing the location of the projector during the performance.

Honeycomb with Queen and Worker Bees

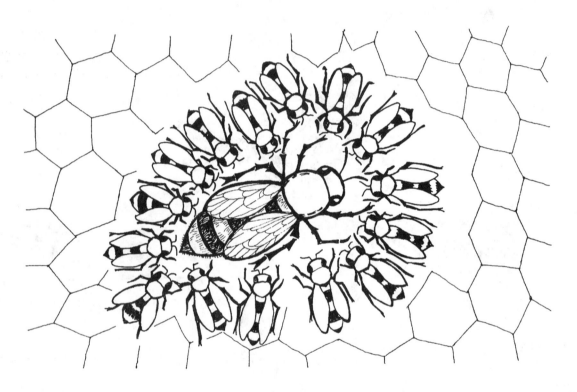

Development of a Bee

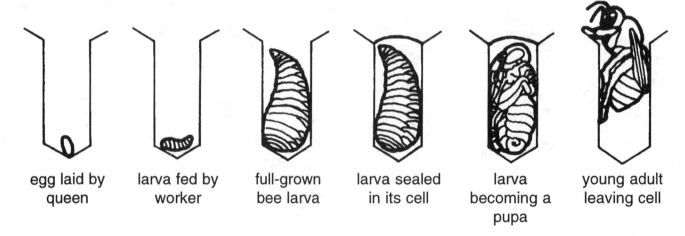

egg laid by queen   larva fed by worker   full-grown bee larva   larva sealed in its cell   larva becoming a pupa   young adult leaving cell

The Story of the Honeybee *(cont.)*

Play Scenery *(cont.)*

Use felt pens to color the meadow scene appropriately. Make a duplicate of the flower field image. Use felt pens to color one copy with yellow petals and orange centers; the other should be blue petals with dark blue centers.

Meadow Scene

Flower Field

Beehive

Beehive Entrance

Dance Pattern

The Story of the Honeybee *(cont.)*

Play Scenery *(cont.)*

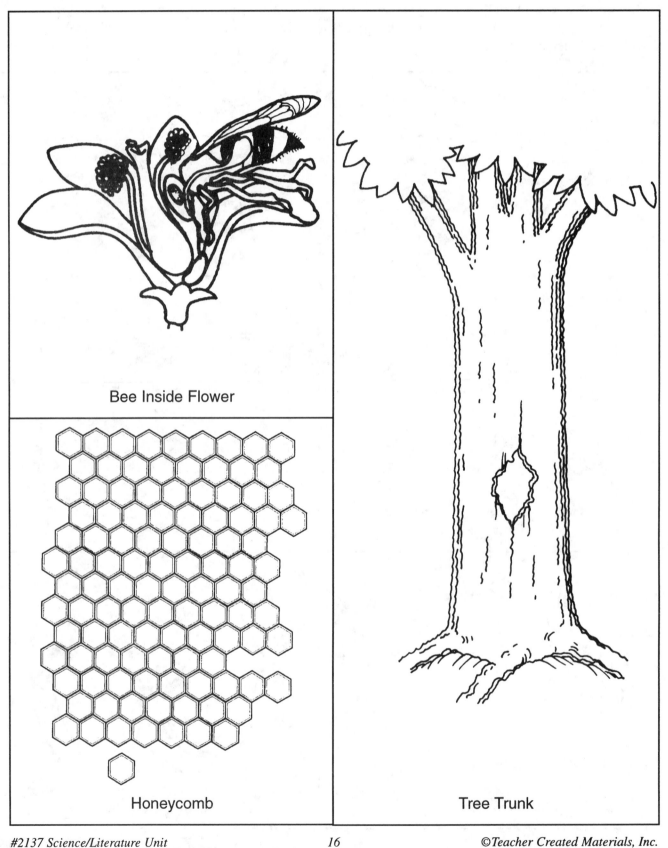

Bee Inside Flower

Honeycomb

Tree Trunk

The Story of the Honeybee *(cont.)*

Play Scenery *(cont.)*

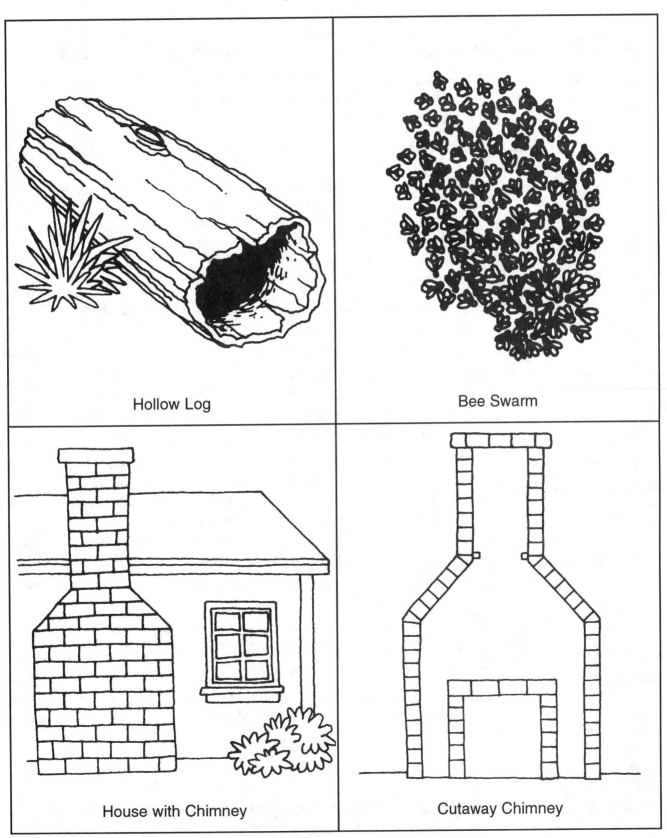

Hollow Log

Bee Swarm

House with Chimney

Cutaway Chimney

The Story of the Honeybee *(cont.)*

Puppet Play Script

Queen Bee:
(cutaway beehive)

Hello and welcome to my home, which is located inside this special box built by human beekeepers. It is called a *hive* and is a perfect place for my entire colony.

(honeycomb with queen and workers)

I'm the queen bee. That's me on the honeycomb. I'm the largest and the most important bee in the hive. I laid all the eggs, and so I am mother to everyone living in this colony. I am really busy laying eggs, now that it's spring. Sometimes I lay as many as 2,000 in one day! I hope you are impressed. There are almost 60,000 of my offspring living in this hive by now. Of course, as a queen bee all I do is eat lots of great honey and lay tens of thousands of eggs. If I'm healthy and well cared for, I could live for five years.

(queen bee puppet, honeycomb)

We are honeybees and live together in a colony, so we are called *social bees*. I want you to meet the bees which really do all the work around this colony. Naturally, they are called *worker bees*.

Worker A: *(queen bee and workers on honeycomb)*

(worker bee puppet)

Hi! I'm Sally, one of the worker bees in this colony. My job is to build and repair the honeycomb. You can see me building it with the help of some of the other worker bees. We make each tubelike cell with six sides, which is a *hexagon,* so they fit snugly together.

I make the wax by eating lots of honey, and then glands in my body turn the sugar in the honey to wax. It oozes out of pores in my abdomen in tiny flakes. I pick off the flakes with my legs and pass them out to my mouth where I can chew them in my strong jaws. Finally, I pack the wax together with my mouth to form the cells.

(Place strip of pictures on projector stage showing development of a bee. Cover all but the pictures showing the queen laying eggs. Gradually uncover the next picture as the script calls for it.)

Queen Bee:
(egg and queen bee puppet in honeycomb cell)

Some of the workers are in charge of the nursery where they take care of the eggs I lay. *(Show queen laying egg in cell.)* First, I lay an egg in each cell of the wax cell honeycomb.

(larva in cell and worker bee puppet)

After three days, a tiny white wormlike larva will hatch from each egg, and the nurse worker bees will feed them.

The Story of the Honeybee *(cont.)*

Puppet Play Script *(cont.)*

Worker B:
(worker puppet)

I'm Martha, one of the nurse bees. You can see me feeding the larva a special diet of brood food which I make with glands in my head. This brood food is creamy and very rich in vitamins and proteins. After three days, I feed the larva a kind of bee bread which is a mixture of honey and pollen.

(pupa in cell)

The larva grows so big it fills the cell.

I seal the cell closed with some wax.

(pupa in cell)

The larva changes into a pupa and goes through a *metamorphosis*, which means a change. Gradually the larva becomes an adult bee.

(adult leaving cell)

The adult bee will chew its way out of the cell and join the work force. We need all the help we can get!

Scout A:
(flying bee puppet, meadow scene)

I'm a scout worker bee which has been sent to find flowers where we can get nectar and pollen for food. I fly in bigger and bigger circles from the hive until I find the flowers. My special eyes will help me see them. I have five eyes! Three tiny ones form a triangle on the top of my head, and two huge bulging eyes are located on each side of my head. Can you see them? These are called compound eyes since they are made up of thousands of lenses packed together. The views from the thousands of lenses in my eyes combine to make one image which is somewhat blurred. My eyes are really great at seeing motion, however.

(yellow flowers and bee puppet)

Look at these flowers I am heading toward. You see them as yellow.

(blue flowers)

I see them like this because I see the ultraviolet light colors in them that you can't see. I can also locate the sun, even if it is a cloudy day. I need to know the sun's location so I can return to the hive and let my sister worker bees know just where to come to collect the food.

I'll fly back to the hive now and do my waggle dance to show them how to find the flowers.

The Story of the Honeybee *(cont.)*

Puppet Play Script *(cont.)*

Guard A:
(hive entrance, three guard puppets)

My name is Maria. I am a guard worker bee, and I make sure nothing comes into the hive except members of my family. These are some of my sisters who help me.

(flying bee, hive entrance)

Look out, here comes a bee now! Come on, girls, we need to use our antennae to see if she smells like us. If she doesn't, we'll have to fight her so she can't invade our hive.

(guards sniffing bee)

You smell OK. Let her pass. Imagine how impossible it would be to know each member of our family by sight since we all look alike. That's why our mother, Queen Cleopatra, passes around a *pheromone,* or scent, to each of us so we all smell alike and we know who belongs in this colony.

Scout A:
(honeycomb with dance pattern on top, top view of bee puppet)

OK, Girls, watch my dance. I'm going to show you just where I discovered the flowers. Now, I'll repeat the dance for you. Notice how I waggle toward the left; that means my sister bees will fly to the left of the sun to find the flowers.

Worker C:
(entrance of hive, bee puppets flying)

I think we know just where to fly now. Follow me, girls. We are really working hard to fly with these heavy bodies of ours. Our wings flap about 250 times per second, and our top speed is 15 mph! We can fly forward, backward, and hover just like a helicopter.

(blue flower field, three flying bee puppets)

There are the flowers! We will use our ultraviolet vision to see just where to land on the flowers to collect nectar.

Worker D:
(bee inside flower)

Watch how I get down inside this flower and use my long tube-like tongue as a straw to drink the nectar into my honey stomach. My body is furry, so I also get covered with the sticky pollen which is on the tips of the stamen inside these flowers. I'll scrape the pollen off and put it into the pollen baskets on my back legs. Can you see the pollen I have already collected? Some of this pollen will fall off when I go to the next flower, but that is good since it helps the flower make seeds which become new plants. You call this process *pollinating* the plants. Bees are about the best pollinators on Earth! Many of the fruits and vegetables you eat depend upon us to continue growing.

(flying bees)

20

The Story of the Honeybee *(cont.)*

Puppet Play Script *(cont.)*

Worker D: *(cont.)* It's time for us to fly back to the hive with our loads of nectar and pollen to pack it into the honeycomb cells.

Guard B:
(entrance with three guard bees) Be alert, girls—incoming bees! We need to give them the sniff test. You smell just right, so you can go inside.

Worker D:
(bees on top of honeycomb) I'll pump up the nectar from my stomach through my tongue into this cell. Now, I'll add some chemical enzymes to it. Other worker bees will fan the nectar to evaporate the water so it will turn into honey. We eat this honey for energy. The beekeeper collects the honey so you can eat it too. There is plenty of honey for all of us.

(bee puppet on comb) I'm shaking the pollen out of the baskets on my hind legs into this cell. This pollen will give us the fat, proteins, vitamins, and minerals we need in our diet. *(Shouting)* Oh no! I smell the banana scent the guard bees give off when there is danger. Bee alert! Everyone to the entrance! We have to help guard the hive!

Guard C:
(wasp and three guard bees at entrance) You're not coming into my hive!

There go two of our brave sisters stinging and killing the wasp. The hooks on the ends of the stingers will make them stay inside the wasp's body. It's sad that our sister bees will die when the stingers are pulled out of their bodies, but they have saved all the rest of us.

Queen Bee:
(honeycomb with queen and workers) Whew! That attack was a close call, but the guards were courageous and saved us.

I've been in this hive for a long time, and it's time for me to leave and start a new home. I'll take a few thousand workers with me to help. There will soon be a new queen bee coming out of one of these cells. The nurse bees have been feeding it a special rich royal jelly so it will become larger and can take over my duties.

(queen bee and worker puppets, hive entrance) Fly with me, we'll find a tree so we can gather and set up a temporary headquarters while the scout bees look for a new location for our colony.

The Story of the Honeybee *(cont.)*

Puppet Play Script *(cont.)*

Worker B:
(larvae in cells and worker bee puppet)

You may have noticed that all the bees you have heard from so far were females.

There are very few males in our colony, and their only job is to mate with a queen so she can produce eggs. The larvae in these cells will become male bees, called *drones*. When they become adults, they will leave the hive to look for a queen from another nest so they can mate with her. After that, their job is done and they will die.

(two guard puppets, dragging one drone out of the entrance)

If there are any leftover drones in our hive when winter comes, the workers will drag them out of the hive. This may sound very cruel, but our food supplies run low in the winter when there are few or no flowers around. The drones can't even feed themselves on flower nectar since their tongues are too short, so we would have to feed them from our stored food during the winter. It is more important to feed it to the worker bees because we keep the rest of the colony members alive.

Scout A:
(bee-swarm in tree, three scout bee puppets)

The scouts have been sent to look for a new home for us. The queen will stay behind with the workers that will protect her during our search. Each of us will look for a different homesite and then return to the swarm and do a dance to show directions to our new locations.

(hollow tree, scout bee flying inside)

Look, I think that would be a good spot! *(The scout should cover her mouth with cupped hands to make it sound as if she is speaking into a hollow area.)* This looks like a great spot in here. I'll return to the swarm to tell the others about it. *(Scout bee flies back to swarm.)*

(Show tree with swarm and place the dance pattern under the picture in the region of the tree trunk. Use the top view of bee puppet to perform the dance.)

Scout A:

This is how you get to the tree I found. Let's go check it out.

The Story of the Honeybee *(cont.)*

Puppet Play Script *(cont.)*

Scout B:
(hollow tree, three bee puppets)

I don't think this will be a safe place for us. We need one which has a smaller entrance so it is easier to protect. Follow me to the one I found in a hollow log.

Scout C:
(hollow log)

(Talk into cupped hands.) This is too close to the ground. It could be invaded by skunks or other insects. Come with me to check out the great place I found.

Scout B:
(house with chimney)

This is a great place! The entrance is small so it's easy to protect, and the wind and rain can't get inside. We can build the nest higher up the chimney so warm air won't escape. It also faces south, so the sun will keep us warm inside here.

Scout A:
(cutaway chimney, bee puppet inside)

(Talk into cupped hands.) The size is just right—large enough to hold the honeycomb we need but not too big for us to keep it warm. I think we should fly back to the swarm and bring the others here.

Scout C:
(swarm of bees laid on projector stage, bee puppets flying)

We have found a perfect place for our new home. Follow me— I'll lead the way.

(Scout flies back to swarm to encourage them to keep together.) Stay together everyone! I'll show you the right way to go.

Queen Bee:
(chimney, bees entering)

(Talk into cupped hands.) Wow! You did a great job. This will make a perfect home for our new colony. Everyone set to work making the honeycomb! I need to get busy laying more eggs to expand my family again.

Flower Power

Shirley, a student in Ms. Frizzle's class, wrote a report titled "Looking for Bee Food? Try a Flower." She showed a cutaway picture of the parts of a flower in her report.

Let's take a flower apart to discover what it looks like.

To the Teacher: Some plants produce two kinds of flowers on the same plant. One will have only *stamens,* the other only *pistils.* These are *incomplete* flowers. There are also *composite* flowers, such as dandelions and marigolds, which have many complete flowers clustered into one.

The flower used for this activity, known as a *complete* flower, should have both stamens and a pistil. These include flowers like the lily, gladiola, tulip, and fruit blossoms. Select the largest flowers for this lesson and provide a variety of blossoms.

Materials: *For the student*—complete flower, data sheets (pages 25 and 26), clear tape, magnifier

                For the teacher—transparency of "How Flowers Reproduce" (page 27), several apples

Procedure

- Distribute the materials to the students and let them follow the data sheet to help them dissect the flowers.

Closure

- Let students discuss what they have learned about the flowers through this activity.

- Use the transparency of "How Flowers Reproduce" to explain the reproduction process to students.

- Tell them bees are the best pollinators of flowers. When the bee goes to the flower to get nectar and pollen, some of the pollen drops off its body onto the sticky stigma on top of the pistil. Other insects which visit flowers also help pollinate them. Pollen can be transferred to the stigma by wind and also by some birds and bats.

- Explain that fruit and vegetables are really the swollen ovaries of the blossoms that grew on the plants. Show the students the example of the apple and point out the leftover blossom and stem on opposite ends. Cut the fruit open to expose the seeds which have formed inside the ovary.

- Tell the students that beekeepers often rent their hives to farmers who have apple orchards or other fruit trees, so they can be pollinated. Let the students eat the apples and examine the seeds. The seeds may be planted to see the development of new apple plants.

Extender: Take students on a walk to search for fruit-bearing plants that show blossoms as well as fruit. Try to find examples of the transition from blossom to fruit on the plant. Cut open one of the blossoms to expose the swollen ovary inside, the beginning of the fruit.

Let students bring in a variety of domestic and wild flowers to dissect and compare with the examples they used. Provide them with some incomplete and composite flowers to examine as well.

Flower Power *(cont.)*

Flower Dissection Instructions

To the Student: Follow the directions as you carefully dissect the flower.

- Snip off a piece of the stem. Examine it with the magnifier and then tape it in the box marked "stem" on the "Parts of a Flower" data sheet. Complete the rest of the information in the box.

- Locate the sepals, petals, stamens, and pistil. Count the number of each and write this in the appropriate boxes.

- Gently pull off the sepals and tape a specimen in the sepal box. Describe how it feels.

- Smell the flower. If it has a fragrance, describe it in the petal box. Carefully remove the petals and tape one to the data sheet. Answer the question about the flower's color and fragrance.

- Examine a stamen, the male part of the flower. Look at the top of the stamen (anther) with a magnifier to see the pollen grains. Put your fingertip against the anther. Does the pollen stick to your finger? This is what happens when a bee touches it. Rub the pollen between your fingers and then describe what it feels like in the pollen box.

- Using the sticky side of a piece of clear tape, lift a sample of pollen grains. If you have a microscope, place the tape on a glass slide and examine it. Put a sample of pollen grains in the pollen box. Draw what the pollen grains look like when magnified.

- Remove the stamens and tape one of them in the box. Describe what you see on the anther and draw a magnified view of it.

- Study the pistil, the female part of the flower. Feel the stigma, the top of the pistil. Describe how it feels. At the bottom of the pistil is a swollen area (ovary). Try to cut it open with your fingernail. Use your magnifier to see if you can find any tiny seeds inside the ovary. You may be able to split the stem of the stigma (*style*) lengthwise to see if you can locate the pollen tube which has grown from the stigma to the ovary.

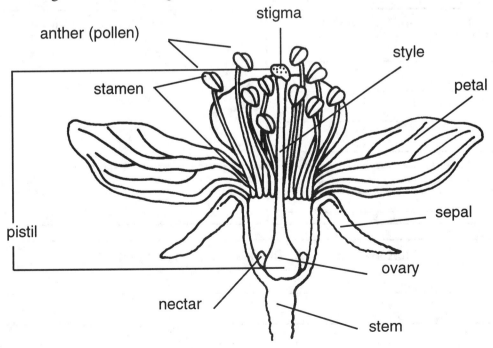

Flower Power *(cont.)*

Parts of a Flower

Stem

Description: _____

_____

_____

_____

Magnified view
of tip of stem:

Sepal

Number of sepals: _____

Description of how it feels:

_____

_____

_____

Petal

Number of petals: _____

Why do flowers have
colored petals and
sometimes have a
fragrance? _____

_____

_____

Pollen

Describe how it feels:

_____

_____

_____

Magnified view
of pollen grains:

Stamen

Number of stamen: _____

Describe what you saw on
the anther: _____

_____

_____

Magnified view
of the anther:

Pistil

Number of pistils: _____

Describe how the stigma
feels: _____

_____

_____

Magnified view
inside the ovary:

Describe how a bee can pollinate flowers.

_____

_____

_____

_____

_____

Bee Pollinating a Flower

What are other ways flowers can be pollinated?

1._____

2._____

3._____

Flower Power *(cont.)*

How Flowers Reproduce

1. Each pollen grain is a single cell. Pollen forms on the top (anther) of the stamen.
2. Pollen is carried by insects, wind, or birds to the stigma—the sticky top of the pistil.
3. Once on the stigma, the pollen grain absorbs moisture from the pistil and breaks open.
4. Its contents form a pollen tube growing down into the pistil.
5. The pollen tube grows until it reaches the ovule containing an egg cell.
6. Sperm from the pollen travels down the tube to the ovule and unites with the egg cell.
7. A seed now begins to develop inside the ovary.
8. An ovary may have a single seed (avocado) or more than one seed (apple).
9. The ovary develops into a fruit enclosing the seed(s).

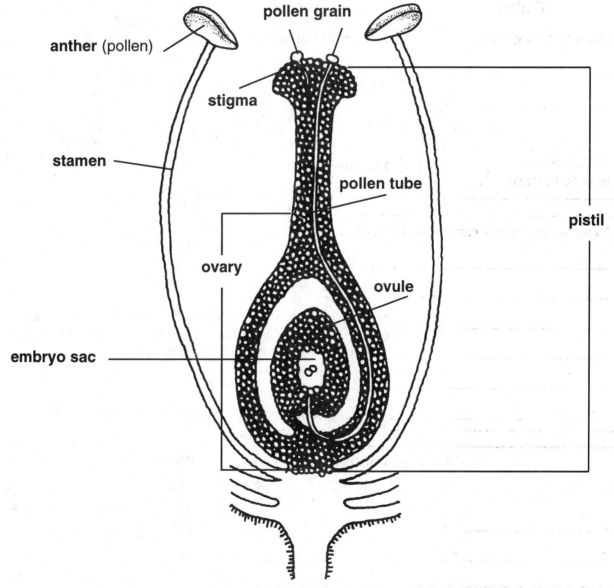

Going on a Bee Hunt

Ms. Frizzle and her students become bees and follow the others from the hive to find nectar and pollen in flowers. Although it isn't possible for you to become a bee, you can go to areas where they will be working hard to collect food for their colony.

Materials: area of flowers, video camera, notepaper

Caution: Before taking this field trip, take into consideration that many students are afraid of bees, especially if they have been stung. There may also be students who are allergic to bee stings. Take precautions by preparing the students well before the trip and dividing them into small groups which are supervised by other adults. You may prefer to arrange to take the students under your supervision in small groups to observe the bees.

Lesson Preparation: Scout the area near the school for flowers which attract bees that students can visit and observe in action. Practice observing the bees so you will be able to tell the students how to do this successfully without disturbing them. Show a video or film which shows close-up images of bees in action so the students will know what to expect (see Resources section).

Take this field trip on a sunny day in the spring when bees are searching for food.

Procedure

- Prepare students for this trip by describing how you observed bees collecting food in the wild by watching carefully and silently at a safe distance.

- Remind the students of what they learned about the bees' vision being blurred but being able to detect motion very well. The bees will ignore the students if they do not make sudden moves or try to touch the bees.

- Discuss what students should look for during the field trip, such as the following:

  1. How the bee approaches and enters the flower, how the wings move
  2. Collection of pollen in the pollen baskets on the hind legs as well as on the body
  3. Noise that the bees' wings may be making
  4. Which flowers the bees seem to like best

- If a video camera is available, take it to the site where the bees are visiting the flowers and videotape the action. Students can view this tape and discuss what they see. Another way to do this is to use a still camera and take a series of pictures for students to examine.

Closure

- After returning to the classroom, redivide the students into groups so they can share the experiences they had with members of other groups.

- List the observations on the board for all students to copy and include in their Insect Folders.

Extender: A good way to let students see that bees are very important is to have a beekeeper come to tell about his or her work. Check the telephone book under "bees" or contact your local nursery to find a beekeeper in your area. It may even be possible to follow this visit with a trip to a real beehive.

The Ants Go Marching

Ms. Frizzle's class studied many types of insects before she decided to take them on their trip to the beehive. Among the insects they studied were ants, which also live in communities like bees. Ants are fascinating to observe in the wild and are easily kept in captivity for closer study.

Ant Facts

Over 2,500 Species . . .

There are over 2,500 species of ants known. All are social animals which live and work together in colonies. They are among the most familiar of insects to humans, and they have often been compared to human societies. Each ant in a colony has specific duties. A single queen ant reproduces all of the colony's members. She may live as long as 20 years! At certain times of the year, queen ants lay eggs that develop into males and young queens that will have wings. A few weeks after these become adults, they leave the colony and go on a mating flight. After mating, the males die and the queen tears off her wings and either returns to her nest as another queen or begins her own nest.

Soldiers Protect . . .

The soldier ants are responsible for protecting the members of the colony. The worker ants are all female and are responsible for the maintenance of the colony. Their jobs range from husking seeds and carrying out dirt to digging new tunnels and feeding the larvae. An ant colony consists of many (sometimes millions) ants working cooperatively to form a single society.

Queen Size . . .

Usually the queen ant is the largest, followed by males and then workers. Among the carpenter ants, some workers are larger than the males. These large workers are called *soldiers*.

Carpenter Ants in a Colony

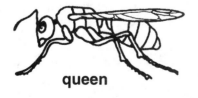
queen

male

worker (normal size)

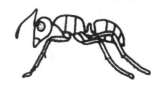
soldier

Ants in the Wild

To the Teacher: This study has been divided into several activities which will be spread over several weeks. Students will gather data as they observe ants in the wild and specimens living in two ant farms.

Materials: pieces of food such as fruit, candy, or meat; popcorn and a popcorn maker

Lesson Preparation: Find a location on the school grounds where ants can be observed, such as a sandbox or dirt area. Spend some time watching the ants to observe them. Scatter some of the food near the ants and draw a line through their trail to watch how they behave.

On the day of this lesson, scatter food near the ant area to attract them if they are not already active. You may want students to bring their chairs so they can sit in small groups near the ants and make careful observations. Consider letting students videotape the ants so they can make closer observations back in the classroom.

Make fresh popcorn and place it in the classroom where it is hidden but where students will smell it as they enter the room.

Procedure

- As the students enter the room and smell the popcorn, ask them to see if they can find it. Once they discover it, serve the popcorn to them.

- Explain that today they will begin a study of ants by visiting them in the wild.

- Take the students to the ant area and divide them into small groups to observe and discuss what they see the ants doing. Tell the students to watch one ant for a few minutes to see how it moves. Ask them to see what happens when one ant meets another. (Sometimes they touch face-to-face, most likely smelling each other.)

- Have them watch the ants' behavior when food is placed near them. Tell them to look to see if the food is carried off and to observe how this is done.

- Look for an uninterrupted trail of ants and make several breaks in the trail by drawing lines through it with a stick at intervals of about six inches. Encourage students to see if they can determine how the ants rediscover the path. Explain that ants have very poor vision, so they cannot see the path. After awhile, remind students of how they found the popcorn in the classroom (by smell). Explain that as the ants travel, they leave a smell behind them on the trail which is followed by the ants behind them. They use their antennae to smell. When the line is drawn across their path, the smell is broken and they need to move around until they find it again.

Closure

- Have students write brief descriptions in their Insect Folders of what they observed the ants doing.

- Be sure they illustrate their essays to give more details.

Ants Close Up

To the Teacher: This lesson should be conducted the day after observing the ants in the wild.

Materials: copies of the Ant Record data sheet (page 32) for each student, transparency of the Ant Record,, spoon, resealable baggy, magnifier for every group of students, transparencies of Ant Facts (page 29), Body Parts of an Ant (page 33), and An Ant Colony (page 34).

Lesson Preparation: Use the spoon to place several ants in the resealable baggies. Blow a bit of air into the bag before sealing it. Staple the baggies closed for the safety of the ants.

Procedure

- Ask students to share their Insect Journal information showing what they learned about ants as they watched them in the wild.

- Place one of the baggies containing live ants on the overhead projector. Let students observe and discuss what they see for a few minutes. Tell the students that they are going to work in groups to observe ants that are inside baggies.

- Divide the students into groups of four and distribute the ants in the baggies to them. Provide a magnifier for each group. Give each student a copy of the Ant Record. Show a copy of the record on the overhead and discuss how students should complete the form.

- Remind students that they are working with live insects which are very small and therefore need to be handled very gently. Explain that following this lesson you will release the ants where they were collected. Caution the students not to try to open the bags, for the safety of the ants. Let them observe their ants in the bag and record these observations on the data sheet.

Closure

- Place one of the baggies on the overhead projector so students can observe it as a class. Have a spokesperson from each group share something he or she noticed about the ants which had not been mentioned at the beginning of this lesson.

- Show and discuss the transparency of the Ant Facts to familiarize students with the types of ants found in the colony.

- Show and discuss the transparency of the ant body parts. Have students compare their drawings to see if they found most of these external parts of the ant.

- Discuss the transparency of the ant colony and point out the chambers of the nest and the different ants shown inside and outside the colony.

- Have students add their drawings and copies of the three ant pictures to their Insect Folders.

Ants Close Up *(cont.)*

Ant Record

Name: _____

Make careful observations of one ant with a magnifier; then draw what you see.

Ant Viewed from Above   **Ant Viewed from the Side**

Describe how your ant walks.

_____

_____

Make a series of drawings to show how the ant moves when walking.

1	2	3	4

Tell what you observed of the ants in the wild. *(Be sure to describe how they reacted to the food.)*

_____

_____

Draw a picture to show one of the ants in action. *(Tell what the ant is doing in your picture.)*

Ants Close Up *(cont.)*

Body Parts of an Ant

External

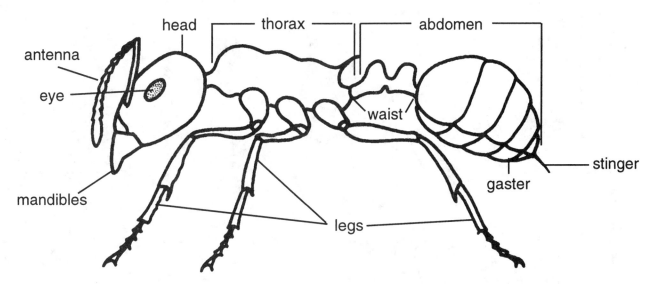

An ant is an insect and therefore has three main body parts (1) the *head*, (2) the *thorax*, and (3) the *abdomen*. The main features of the head are the *eyes, antennae,* and *mandibles* (jaws). Three pairs of legs are attached to the thorax. The narrow front part of the abdomen is called the *waist*. Some ants have a stinger at the tip of the abdomen.

Internal

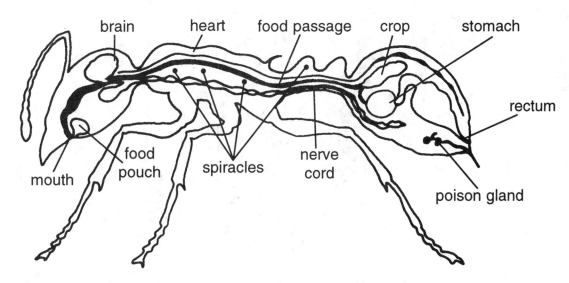

An ant's internal organs include a brain and nerve cord and a tubelike heart. The ant breathes through *spiracles,* which are tiny openings along the sides of its body. Its digestive system includes a food pouch that squeezes the liquid out of food. The liquid moves through a food passage to the crop, a storage pouch, and then to the stomach, where digestion occurs. Wastes pass through the rectum and out of the body. Only ants with stingers have the poison glands at the top of their abdomen.

Ants Close Up *(cont.)*

An Ant Colony

queen and males flying off to mate

bringing in food

carrying husks to throw away outside

husking seeds

storing seeds

sharing food

carrying dirt out of the nest

workers with larvae

workers with pupae

carrying eggs to nurseries

queen with workers

worker resting

This is the inside of the harvester ant colony. The nest has many rooms connected by tunnels. The tunnels reach throughout the ant mound and deep underground. One chamber is the queen's home where she is fed and cared for by the worker ants. She will lay her eggs here, and the worker ants will carry them to other rooms which are nurseries. The workers will take care of the ant larvae until they become adults. Some chambers are gathering or resting places for the workers. Harvester ants also have rooms for storing seeds which they collect from outside the nest. The ants spend the winter in the deepest rooms of their nest.

During mating season, male ants and the new queen ants grow wings and move outside to mate. The queen will tear off her wings after mating and return to the nest or move elsewhere to begin a colony of her own. The males will die after the mating season.

Inside the Ant Farm

To the Teacher: Insect Lore (see Resources section, page 48) supplies ant farms of various sizes that include an ant watcher's manual, sand, and a coupon to return for a supply of live ants. Two regular sized ant farms should be purchased for this activity (if funds are available) to have students work in smaller groups and have the opportunity to compare two ant colonies.

Caution: *Do not add wild ants to those already in the ant farms; they will kill each other.*

Materials: one or two commercial ant farms with live ants and instructions for assembling ant farm, Ant Record (made during earlier study of wild ants), lined paper, video camera (optional)

Lesson Preparation: Order the ant farms early enough to allow time to send in the coupon for the live specimens. Assemble the ant farm(s) with the exception of the ants. Label the respective sides of the ant farm A and B for observations.

Procedure

- Arrange the students so they will be able to see the ant farms. Have them discuss their Ant Records to tell what they have learned about ants during their observations of them in the wild. Tell them that ants live beneath the ground in colonies which are much bigger than we can see from the surface.

- Explain that they will be able to observe what goes on beneath the ground in an ant colony by watching the ant farms over the next several weeks. Show them the live ants which were supplied for the farm. Explain that these are all worker ants; no queen ant is included. Let the students look at the ants so they can compare them with those they saw in the wild.

- Follow the instructions provided by the distributor for placing the ants and food into the farm(s).

- Let the students begin to observe what they see happening. Discuss their observations, drawing their attention to areas of interest. Permit them to observe the ants long enough to see how the ants settle into their new home.

Closure

- Distribute lined paper to each student and have them write a letter to someone at home, telling about this special event. Encourage them to add drawings to help the reader understand what they observed.

- Permit them to take the letters home and later add them to their Insect Folder.

Extender: A time-lapse video record of the changes in one ant farm can be produced by recording just a minute or two of tape daily. Mark the location of the ant farm and the camera position so they will be in the same spot every time. Always tape the exact same section of the ant farm and take some closeup shots to show details. The final video will show the changes as a continuous sequence. This will enrich student understanding and observations.

Inside the Ant Farm *(cont.)*

To the Teacher: Conduct this lesson on the day following the introduction of the ant farm.

Materials: data sheet—Ant Farm Observations (page 37), books about ants (see Resources sections page 48), colored pens or pencils, magnifying lenses

Teacher Information: Once the ants have begun to tunnel into the sand of the ant farm, have students begin to make observations and record them for their Insect Journals.

Lesson Preparation: Set the ant farms in two different locations so students can sit and make their observations each day. Schedule student observations in small groups so they can observe the ants for about 10 minutes daily. The ant farms should **not** be moved once the ants begin their tunnels. If the ant farm is moved, tunnels may give way and trap the ants.

Procedure

- Tell the students they are scientists who will carefully observe the changes in the ant farm every day.

- Show the students where the ant farm(s) have been placed in the classroom for their observation. If more than one ant farm is used, divide the students between them.

- Post and explain the schedule for their observations.

- Tell why the ant farms should not be moved.

- Distribute a copy of the Ant Farm Observations data sheet to each student and discuss how they will record the daily changes they see. Explain the use of different colored pens or pencils to record changes in the tunnels.

- Let the first group of students go to the ant farms and begin their records. Monitor their progress to be sure they are making detailed drawings.

Closure

- Let the students continue their observations for about two weeks.

- Read a book that describes an ant colony and share the illustrations with the students.

Extender: The diagram of an ant colony on page 34 shows a group of harvester ants. Entomologists (scientists who study insects) tell us that there are about 20, 000 species of ants which they classify in a number of different ways. As student scientists, your class may wish to divide into groups to investigate and report on the behavior, appearance, physical qualities, geographical range, and species, of the following types of ants: harvester ants, honey ants, dairying ants, army ants, fungus growers, and slave makers.

Inside the Ant Farm *(cont.)*

Ant Farm Observations

Name: _____

To the Student: Observe the ant farm for at least two weeks, making drawings to show the changes you see. Add the changes in the tunnels to the last drawings in pencil, and then trace over them with colored pen or pencil. Use a different color each day and record that day's color on the key by coloring the circle beside the date. If there is no change, record the date and write "no change" in the color column. Record both sides of the ant farm each day.

Key

Date   Color

_____ ○
_____ ○
_____ ○
_____ ○
_____ ○
_____ ○
_____ ○

Ant Farm Side A

A

Key

Date   Color

_____ ○
_____ ○
_____ ○
_____ ○
_____ ○
_____ ○
_____ ○

Ant Farm Side B

B

Make notes below of interesting things you see happen. Be sure to include the dates of these observations. If you need more space for your notes, use another piece of lined paper.

_____

_____

Inside the Ant Farm *(cont.)*

To the Teacher: This experiment should be conducted about one week after beginning the ant farm, when the tunnels are well underway.

The dark side of the ant farm should encourage the ants to make more tunnels on that side than on the other, since wild colonies are underground and therefore mostly in the dark.

Materials: ant farm(s), black construction paper, Ant Farm Observations data sheet (page 37), transparency of the Life Cycle of an Ant (page 39)

Lesson Preparation: Cover one side of the ant farm(s) with black paper so no light can enter. Let the cover remain on during a weekend or at least for two full days.

Procedure

* Explain that an experiment will be conducted on the ant farm by covering one side of it so no light can enter. Tell the students that after two days the black paper will be removed, and they will look for any changes in the tunnels.

* Have students write what they think might happen to the covered side of the tunnel.

* After the cover has been in place for two days, remove it and have students record what the tunnels look like by adding new drawings to the Ant Farm Observations data sheet. They should make the record of new tunnels in pencil and then trace over it with colored pen to show these new additions.

Closure

* Let students compare the results of the experiment with their original predictions. Then have them explain why changes may (or may not) have occurred on the dark side of the colony.

* The ants in the ant farm will not go through a complete life cycle since there is no queen.

* If they have ever seen a nest disturbed, students may have seen ants trying to rescue the eggs in their colony.

* Show the transparency of the life cycle of the ant and give a copy to the students to include in their Insect Folder.

Extender: Cover the same side of the ant farm for two or more days and then remove it for observations and record the new changes.

Life Cycle of an Ant

Ants develop in four stages: (1) *egg,* (2) *larva,* (3) *pupa,* and (4) *adult.* The queen ant lays all the eggs in the colony. These hatch within a few days into larvae. During the larval stage, the ants are like white worms which do not move about. This stage lasts about three weeks. In some species, the larvae spin cocoons before becoming pupae.

The pupa is also colorless and does not eat or move. During the pupal stage, the ant gradually becomes an adult. This stage lasts about two to three weeks before the black adult ant emerges.

The queen may lay thousands of eggs in her lifetime. Most of the eggs will be workers. After the colony is well developed, the queen lays eggs which will become males and queens.

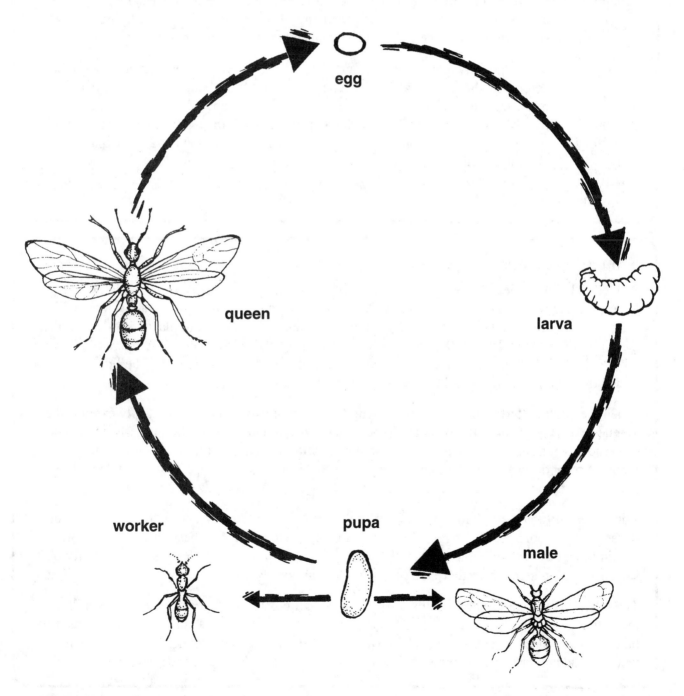

egg

larva

queen

worker

pupa

male

Raising Painted Lady Butterflies

Ms. Frizzle's class discovers that each bee begins life as an egg, which hatches into a larva, then becomes a pupa, and finally changes to an adult. This method of development is called *metamorphosis*. Raising painted lady butterfly larvae in captivity is an exciting way to study this gradual change into a very different looking adult insect.

Painted Lady Butterfly Facts

Throughout the world . . .

Painted lady butterflies are found throughout the world. They eat the mallow (malva) or hollyhock leaves, which are weeds. They can frequently be seen in early spring, flying in large groups after just emerging from their chrysalides and migrating to new areas.

The larva hatches from a tiny, pale green egg and then begins to feed. As the larva grows, it sheds its tight skin (a process called *molting*) and leaves it in a black furry ball. About 10 days after hatching, the larva hangs upside down and prepares to become a pupa. After 24 hours, the caterpillar's skin splits, and the chrysalis, which has formed under the skin, wiggles free. Within about four hours the chrysalis hardens. The adult emerges in seven to ten days and expands its wings with fluid pumped from its abdomen. The wings take about an hour to harden before the butterfly can take flight. Some red fluid may be expelled; this is waste material accumulated during the pupa stage.

Easy to raise . . .

Painted lady butterflies are easy to raise. The larva and food are available commercially (see Resources section). Small plastic vials with lids are supplied, one for each larva. Malva leaf paste is sent with the larva and is divided among the vials. The larvae are placed inside, and then the vials are capped. The containers are kept in a well-lighted area where the temperature is 75°–80°F (24°–27°C). Each larva will form its chrysalis on the lid of its vial. The lid can then be transferred into an enclosure where the adult will eventually emerge.

When the adult butterfly first emerges, its long tongue is in two parts. The butterfly extends the tongue several times until the parts are joined lengthwise into a hollow tube. It curls up outside the head when not in use. In the wild, the butterfly will drink nectar through this strawlike mouth. In captivity, it can drink juice from pieces of fruit such as orange or watermelon. These may be placed on the bottom of the butterfly enclosure and replaced every two days.

Butterflies will mate after emerging, and the females may begin to lay eggs within five to seven days after they emerge. The eggs will hatch in three to five days. It is best to free the butterflies within three days of their emerging so the eggs can be laid in the wild. Release the butterfly on a sunny day in an area where there are plants, preferably weeds.

The release is a great event, and all students should participate. If they sit or stand very still as the butterflies are released, they may be treated to having one of them land on them. It is as if the butterflies are bidding their "parents" farewell before flying off to make their own way in the world. Students may see the butterflies in the area for several days after the release.

40

Recording Larvae Growth

To the Teacher: Students will keep daily growth records of the painted lady larvae as they grow. This will be done by measuring and drawing them. This takes place during five to nine days from the day the larvae arrive.

Materials: 30 live painted lady butterfly larvae, vials with lids and nutrient, two paper towels, copies of data sheet—Painted Lady Butterfly Larva Record (page 42), metric ruler, magnifier

Lesson Preparation: Use the lid from a butterfly larva vial to draw 30 circles on the paper towels. Cut the circles out to be placed inside the lids. Using a pencil, number each paper circle (1–30). Distribute nutrient into the vials and then carefully transfer one larva into each of them. Put the paper circle (numbered side should be visible through the vial) and then a lid over the top of each container. If there are no holes in the lids, use a pin to poke about five holes in each. Use a permanent felt pen and label each lid with the same number as the paper inside the lid.

Procedure

- Distribute a vial and record sheet to each student. Have them complete this data sheet with their names and vial numbers. They should write today's date below one of the vial drawings.

- To prevent contaminating the containers, have students measure the larva as accurately as possible without opening the vial. Calculate growth beginning with the second record.

- Finally, students draw their larvae, using a magnifier to view the details of legs, feet, and heads. The drawings should be life-size and show the larva's locations inside each vial.

Closure

- Students will keep daily records of each larva until it becomes a pupa. Have them compare the growth of the larva with those of other students in the class.

- Let them calculate and record the differences between each day's growth.

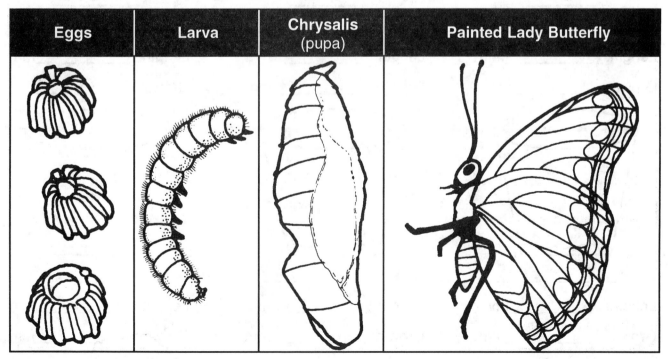

Eggs	Larva	Chrysalis (pupa)	Painted Lady Butterfly

Recording Larvae Growth *(cont.)*

Painted Lady Butterfly Larva Record

Student Name: _____   Vial # _____

To the Student: Measure and record your butterfly larva each day without removing the lid of the vial.

Date: _____

Length: _____mm

Date: _____

Length: _____mm

Growth: _____mm

Date: _____

Length: _____mm

Growth: _____mm

Date: _____

Length: _____mm

Growth: _____mm

Date: _____

Length: _____mm

Growth: _____mm

Date: _____

Length: _____mm

Growth: _____mm

Date: _____

Length: _____mm

Growth: _____mm

Date: _____

Length: _____mm

Growth: _____mm

Date: _____

Length: _____mm

Growth: _____mm

Recording Larvae Growth *(cont.)*

Getting to Know Your Larva

Student Name: _____   Vial # _____

To the Student: Use your magnifier to see the details of your painted lady larva and complete the information below:

1. Look at the bristles which are called setae (*sē tē*) on the caterpillar (larva).

   What color are they? _____

   Are there little setae coming out of the bigger ones? _____

   Draw a large picture of one seta here.

2. Why do you think the larva has setae? _____

   _____

3. Look at the legs of your larva. How many does it have? _____

4. Are the legs exactly alike? _____

   Draw the legs on the right places on the larva outline below:

Painted Lady Butterfly Larva

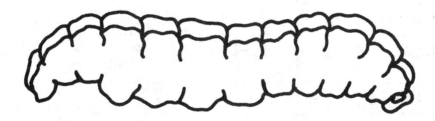

5. Draw the mouth parts of the larva below. Use your magnifier to make this picture large enough to show the details.

Larva Mouth Parts

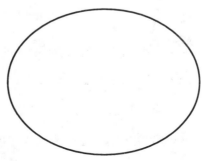

Recording Larvae Growth *(cont.)*

How Does Your Larva Grow?

Student Name: _____   Vial # _____

To the Student: Make a graph using the data you collected on the Painted Lady Butterfly Larva Record. Write the dates for this study along the bottom of the graph, including weekends and holidays. Plot the data on the graph. Connect the dots when all data has been entered.

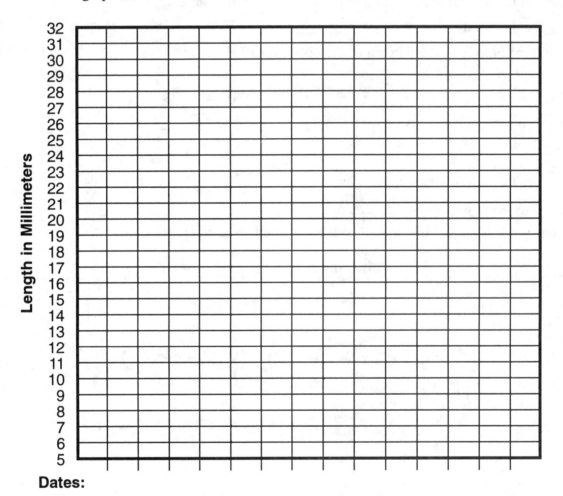

Dates:

Graph Summary

List the dates when you did not measure the larva. Use your graph to find this missing data and record it.

Date	Larva Size from Graph
_____	_____ mm
_____	_____ mm
_____	_____ mm

Use the graph to find between which dates your larva grew most rapidly: _____ and _____

Chrysalis to Butterfly

To the Teacher: Once each larva has formed a chrysalis, it should be carefully transferred to a butterfly enclosure. Students will draw their chrysalides and keep a record of them throughout the period of their development. Hopefully, they will witness the emergence of at least one of the butterflies.

Materials: two pairs of 12" (30 cm) embroidery hoops (available at most craft shops), 1.5 yards (1.4 m) netting 45" (114 cm) wide from a fabric store, 12" (30 cm) diameter circle of cardboard, Butterfly Chrysalis Record data-capture sheet

Directions for making butterfly enclosure:

The butterfly enclosure will look like a tube of net gathered at top and bottom and held open at each end by the embroidery hoops.

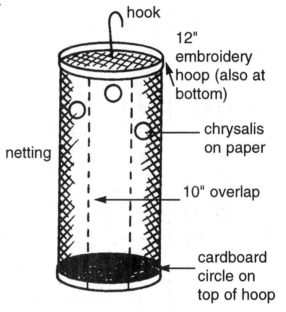

- Work on a large table with an assistant to help you.

- Lay the netting flat on the table and fold it lengthwise so it forms a 10" (25 cm) overlap.

- Tie heavy string or yarn around the netting about 6" (15 cm) from each end to form the tube.

- Insert the inner hoop from one pair of hoops inside the net tube as close to the top as possible.

- Place the outer hoop over this one on the outside of the net tube to secure the hoop to the net.

- Place the other hoop at the bottom of the tube.

- Bend a large paper clip into a hook from which to suspend the tube.

- Have someone else hold the net tube up while you adjust the hoops so the tube hangs straight.

- Place the tagboard circle inside the net tube at the bottom where it can rest on the hoop.

Procedure: Remove the chrysalis from the vial, being careful not to dislodge it from the paper. Pin the paper to the inside of the net tube, keeping the chrysalis side out. Use toothpicks to keep the overlap area closed to prevent the butterflies from escaping.

Make several enclosures so the chrysalides can be divided among them. This will enable the students to make closer observations of their pupae. The butterfly should begin to emerge about seven to ten days after it becomes a pupa. Students should watch their chrysalides daily and notice how they begin to darken just before emerging. Have them complete the data sheet, which will help them look for details. The chrysalides should not be removed or handled.

Closure: When the butterflies begin to emerge, have all the students gather to watch the process, including the filling of the butterfly wings with fluid. Watch as the butterflies extend and curl their tongues, gluing the two halves together.

Chrysalis to Butterfly *(cont.)*

Butterfly Chrysalis Record

Student Name: _____   Vial # _____

To the Student: Use a magnifier to look carefully at your chrysalis. Make a large drawing of the chrysalis below. Draw the antennae, eyes, wings, legs, and abdomen, which you can see through the skin of the chrysalis. Be sure to label these parts on your drawing.

> **Painted Lady Chrysalis**

- Carefully color the chrysalis as close to its real colors as possible.

- When the chrysalis is about seven days old, it will turn dark. What do you suppose this means?

_____

- When the chrysalis turns dark, look for the wings and see if you can detect the colors of the wings through the thin shell. What colors do you see? _____

- What is the date you first began your observations of the larva?_____

- When did the chrysalis become a butterfly?_____

- From the larva stage, how many days did it take the larva to become a butterfly?_____

- Draw a picture of your beautiful butterfly below:

> **My Painted Lady Butterfly**

Becoming an Insect

To the Student: Pretend you awaken one morning to discover that you have become one of the insects you have just studied. Decide whether you are a honeybee, ant, or butterfly, and then make drawings and write descriptions of your pictures.

This is what I look like.

_____

_____

_____

_____

This is my home.

_____

_____

_____

_____

I am eating my meal.

_____

_____

_____

_____

1

4

2

3

This is my life cycle.

Related Books and Periodicals

Bosak, Susan. *Science Is* . . . Scholastic Canada LTD., 1991. This is an outstanding source book which offers fascinating facts as well as valuable projects and activities.

Cole, Joanna. *The Magic School Bus® Inside a Beehive.* Scholastic, Inc., 1996. Ms. Frizzle takes her students on another science field trip adventure. This time they become bees and investigate a beehive firsthand.

Dimensional Nature Portfolio Series, Workman Pub., 708 Broadway, New York, NY, 1991. The series includes *The Bees* and *The Butterflies,* each book containing beautiful illustrations and interesting information, enhanced by pop-up representations of the insects.

Faulkner, David K. *Killer Bee Handbook.* Nature Connection, 10839 Charboro Pt., Suite 200, San Diego, CA 92131-1505. A compilation of interesting, accurate information about the Africanized honeybee (killer bees), this gives suggestions for how to prepare for killer bees in your area.

Fischer-Nagel, A&H. *An Ant Colony.* Carolrhoda, Minneapolis, MN, 1989. The book describes the life cycle and community of an ant colony.

Imes, Rick. *The Practical Entomologist.* Simon and Schuster, New York, NY, 1992. This is a great resource covering topics on insect anatomy, behavior, life cycles, how to collect and house insects.

Macquitty, Miranda. *Amazing Bugs.* DK Publishing, New York, NY, 1996. This is an excellent resource book with great pictures showing insect physiology and information about their habits.

Morgan, Sally. *Butterflies, Bugs, and Worms.* Kingfisher, New York, NY, 1996. This is well illustrated, easy to read, and filled with interesting information and activity ideas.

Mound, L. *Eyewitness Books*: *Insects.* Alfred A. Knopf., New York, NY, 1990. This contains general information about the behavior, life cycle, and anatomy of insects. It discusses the important role insects play in Earth's ecology, including beautiful color photographs of rare and exotic species.

Woelfleing, L. *The Ultimate Bug Book.* Western, New York, NY, 1993. Here is a pop-up book containing extraordinary creatures that catch you by surprise. It includes some general facts and characteristics of insects.

Related Materials
(Call for free catalogs.)

Acorn Naturalists, 17300 East 17th St., J-236, Tustin, CA 92680 (800)422-8886. Supplies nature books for all ages, including those about ants and butterflies.

Carolina Biological Supply Co., 2700 York Rd., Burlington, NC 27215 (800)334-5551. Supplies materials about insects, including books, live specimens, puppets, and habitat equipment.

Delta Education, P.O. Box 3000, Nashua, NH 03061-3000 (800)442-5444. Supplies books, videos, magnifying "bug boxes," ant farms, and other insect materials.

Insect Lore, P.O. Box 1535, Shafter, CA 93263 (800)LIVE BUG. Supplies painted lady butterfly larvae, ant farms, silkworm eggs, live ladybird beetles, books, and videos.